A Path of Hope

A Path of Hope

Last Writings of
Brother Roger of Taizé

Brother Roger of Taizé

continuum

Continuum

The Tower Building
11 York Road
London SE1 7NX

80 Maiden Lane
Suite 704
New York, NY 10038

www.continuumbooks.com

English language edition first published 2006 by Continuum.

British Library Cataloguing-in-Publication Data
A catalogue record for this book is available from the British Library.

ISBN 0 8264 9327 0

Typeset by BookEns Ltd, Royston, Herts.
Printed and bound by Ashford Colour Press Ltd, Hampshire

Contents

Contents

Contents

Note

This volume brings together the two short books that the founder of the Taizé Community had completed just before his violent death in August 2005, with the unfinished letter to young people that he was preparing at the time.

The first part, *A Glimmer of Happiness*, was published in French under the title *Pressens-tu un bonheur?* The second part, *Praying in Silence of Heart – One hundred prayers*, was published as *Prier dans le silence du cœur*. The Unfinished Letter (*Lettre inachevée*) was published as the special 2006 edition of *The Letter from Taizé*.

A Glimmer of Happiness

I

God Wants Happiness for Us

There is happiness in giving oneself

If we could know that a life of happiness is possible – even in hours of darkness ...

For a life to be beautiful, it is not really necessary to have exceptional abilities or special skills; there is a happiness in giving oneself.

What makes for a happy existence is to head towards simplicity: simplicity of our heart and of our life.

When simplicity is deeply linked to kind-heartedness, human beings can create a space of hope around them.

For those who move forward from one beginning to another, a life of happiness takes shape. Day by day, and even by night, we shall go to the wellspring: sparkling there in the depths is living water.

Is this, then, what the human soul could be: the secret heartbeat of a happiness?

God's call

God wants happiness for us! But he never invites us to be indifferent to the suffering of others. When we are faced by trials, God encourages us to be creators.

Our life finds meaning when it is the living response to

3

a call from God. But how can we discern God's call? Many people ask, 'What does God want from me?'

In inner silence this answer can well up: 'Dare to give your life for others; there you will find meaning for your existence.'

God wants us to be a reflection of his presence, bearers of a Gospel hope.

All who respond to this call remain aware of their own frailties, but they keep these words of Christ in their hearts: 'Do not be afraid, only trust!'[1]

There are people who sense that God's call for them is a vocation for their entire lifetime. Some have already glimpsed this call in their childhood.

The Holy Spirit has the strength to sustain a 'yes' for our whole life. Has he not placed in human beings a desire for eternity and the infinite?

In the Spirit, again and again, it is possible to find new momentum and to say to ourselves, 'Be steadfast of heart, and keep going forward!' And we can make this discovery: it is sometimes in demanding situations that human beings become fully themselves.

And then, by his mysterious presence, the Holy Spirit brings about a change in our hearts, rapidly for some, imperceptibly for others. What had been obscure and disturbing starts to become clear.

Until the end of our days, daring to say 'yes' can bring so much clarity.

This 'yes' is transparent trust. It is the love in all our loving.

A Glimmer of Happiness

When things are too easy we cannot create

When I was very young, my family would read aloud stories about a group of religious sisters of the seventeenth century. I was captivated to discover what a few women living in community were able to accomplish. I asked myself: if those few women, giving their lives for Christ, had such an impact in communicating the Gospel, could not a few men together in community do the same thing?

Later on, during a convalescence from tuberculosis involving a long relapse, I used to read and meditate. And gradually I realized that it was essential to create a community of men in which each one could give his entire life, with the courage always to keep going forward.

In the summer of 1940, at the beginning of the Second World War, having recovered from my illness I spent a few days in the mountains and there I said to myself, 'You have thought a lot about it; now it's time to begin.'

I wished first of all somehow to test myself: am I able to persevere in the midst of the greatest trials of the day? I wanted to find a house where I could offer hospitality to those who were seeking refuge on account of the war, and where one day there would be a community.

Almost no trains were running, so I left Geneva by bicycle. Some bridges were down; I had to cross the Rhône by a rope bridge, my bicycle on my back.

Already the first morning, not far from the Swiss border, I discovered a house near Frangy in Savoy, a beautiful manor house with a large farm. There was a chapel attached where Saint Francis de Sales had celebrated Mass. The elderly woman who owned it wished to go and live in the village, close to the church; that way, she said, when she was confined to bed she would still hear Mass being celebrated. She was ready to lease her property in return for a small monthly rent.

That place seemed too comfortable to me. I was possessed by a deep conviction: very often, when things are too easy, it is not possible to create.

I continued my journey, and found myself a few days later in the region of Mâcon. Acquainted with the history of Cluny I wanted to visit the place. I expected to find the ruins of the monastery in the midst of a clearing. But Cluny was a small town, and there was a notary there. He spoke to me about a house ten kilometres away. I got on my bicycle and arrived at Taizé late that morning.

The house had been empty for several years. Nobody had made an offer to purchase it. The farmland had been sold; all that was left was an enclosed area near the house.

The life of the village, around the small Romanesque church tower, was simple. There was no running water or telephone service. A neighbour explained to me that there was no place to eat, but she and her daughter would share a meal with me. During the meal, they said to me, 'Stay here; we are so alone, so isolated.' Those words were decisive.

I went back to Cluny to see the notary. He tried to discourage me from going through with the sale. 'You are only twenty-five,' he said, 'and that property is in such bad shape. You may well have to spend part of your life working just to keep it up.' I went to pray for a few moments in the church of Cluny and I decided to choose Taizé.

'Christ Jesus, why did I stop in Taizé? First and foremost to live from you and through you.

'You know that my desire on that day has remained the same today.

'Who did I come to search for but you, Christ?'

A call for life

If Christ were to ask us, 'Who am I for you?',[2] we could reply:

'You are the one who loves us into the life that has no end. You comprehend everything in us. We would like to be utterly transparent with you and give you not just a part but all of our life.'

And since Christ understands everything in us, some people may find themselves telling him:

'The days passed and I did not respond to your call. I went so far as to ask myself: do I really need God? Hesitations and doubts made me drift far from you.

'But even when I remained far from you, you were waiting for me. You remained close to me.

'Day by day, you renew within me the spontaneity which allows me to hold true in a "yes". You look at me with such understanding that my "yes" will be able to carry me onward until my last breath.'

From the beginnings of our community we were aware of the hesitations that could arise in us, those times when the 'yes' and the 'no' clash. And we asked ourselves: how are we going to persevere in the call that God addresses to us?

I wrote a text about our searching and I cannot forget a conversation I had with a woman who had read it. I had a lot of esteem for her. Disabled from birth, she was a writer and had extensive knowledge of the New Testament. She told me, 'Are you afraid you will not be able to persevere? But the Holy Spirit is present, and the Spirit is strong enough to support a vocation for an entire lifetime.'

Gradually, my brothers and I realized that the Holy Sprit was always present and would lead us on the way.

And it became evident that, in order to remain faithful, we had to commit ourselves for our whole lives. We made that commitment for life at Easter 1949. We were seven brothers.

Those who seek communion in God let some of the most luminous words in the New Testament constantly echo within them: 'God did not give us a spirit of fear, but a spirit of love.'[3]

A prospect of happiness? Yes, God wants happiness for us! And there is happiness in the humble giving of oneself.

Holy Spirit, you want joy, the happiness of the Gospel, for each one of us. And the peace of our hearts can make life beautiful for those around us.

The Wonder of a Joy

Unhoped-for joy

A long time before Christ, a believer expressed this invitation: 'Leave your sadness behind; let God lead you to joy.'[4]

When hesitations, or even doubts, take away God's joy in us, we should not worry. Often they are only gaps of unbelief, nothing more.

However murky or opaque our being, the humble, the quite humble trusting of faith wafts through us like a current of life.

And this prayer can come to birth: 'Jesus Christ, inner Light, do not let my darkness speak to me!'[5] These words were written in the fourth century by a Christian from North Africa, Saint Augustine, after several of those close to him died.

When our darkness begins to speak to us, we are caught up in a dizzying spiral.

Are we going through periods when everything appears to be all dried up? With almost nothing a desert flower can blossom, unhoped-for joy.

The joy of forgiveness

What is amazing in the Gospel is forgiveness – the forgiveness that God gives us, and the forgiveness God asks us to give one another.

There is no will to punish in God.

If we could entrust everything to God, even our worries … Then we realize that we are loved by him, comforted, healed.

The Gospel contains breathtaking words: 'Love your enemies; pray for those who hurt you.'[6]

To love and to forgive: there we find one of the wellsprings of joy.

When we forgive, our life begins to change. All forms of severity are replaced by unlimited goodness.

All who strive to root their lives in forgiveness seek to listen rather than to convince, to understand rather than to impose themselves.

As for me, when I was young, at a time when there were so many conflicts across the world, I kept on asking myself: why all these judgements, these oppositions between people and even between Christians?

Then one day – I can still remember the date – in the subdued light of a late summer evening, with darkness settling over the countryside, I said to myself: begin with yourself; resolve never to judge others harshly. Seek to understand rather than to be understood, and you will find joy. I was about seventeen. That day, I had the hope that the resolution I had made was for life.

A shining hope

The Gospel offers such a shining hope that it can bring joy to our soul.

This hope is like a path of light that opens up in our depths. It brings new vitality, even in situations that seem to be heading nowhere.

If there are times when joy begins to fade away, hope can be renewed when we entrust ourselves quite humbly to God.

There is a force that dwells within us, the mysterious presence of the Holy Spirit who whispers in our hearts, 'Surrender yourself to God in all simplicity; the little faith you have is enough.'

But who is this Holy Spirit? He is the one Jesus the Christ promised in Saint John's Gospel: 'I will never abandon you. I will send you the Holy Spirit, who will support and comfort you. He will remain with you for ever.'[7]

Do we think we are alone? The Holy Spirit is there. That presence is invisible, yet it never leaves us. The Spirit is the breath of God, always offered. Like the wind, we do not see it, but we can feel it passing. The Spirit comes to deliver us from discouragement, restoring a zest for life to those who are losing it.

Joy even in trials

How can we remain joyful when, close to us, some people are going through incomprehensible trials?

An Orthodox theologian, Olivier Clément, replies, 'The joy of the Risen Christ is not going to make us insensitive to the suffering of other people. On the contrary, it can make us even more sensitive, and we will be able both to carry this great joy within us and to enter profoundly into the distress and suffering of our neighbour at the same time. There is no contradiction:

joy is not opposed to compassion. I would even go so far as to say that joy nourishes compassion.'[8] In the Gospel, Christ never invites us to sadness. On the contrary, he calls us even to jubilation in the Holy Spirit.[9]

A young African who spent a year at Taizé explained one day how he gradually came to discover joy in the wake of great misfortune. When he was seven years old, his father was killed. And his mother had to flee far away. He said:

'I had not known my parents' love since childhood. So I sought an inner joy, hoping it would give me strength in that suffering. It enabled me to leave loneliness behind. Joy changes everyday relationships.'

Joy and kind-heartedness

I asked a young man one day what he felt was most essential for him to keep going in life. His reply was: 'Joy and kind-heartedness.'

Worry and the fear of suffering can take away joy.

When a joy drawn from the Gospel wells up in us, it brings with it a breath of new life.

We are not the ones who create this joy; it is a gift of the Holy Spirit. It is constantly renewed by the look of trust with which God regards our life.

Kind-heartedness is not gullible; it requires us to be vigilant. It can lead us to take risks. It leaves no room for looking down on others.

It makes us attentive to the most destitute, to those in distress, to the suffering of children. It lets us show, by the look on our face or by the tone of our voice, that every human being needs to be loved.

During a visit to Taizé the philosopher Paul Ricoeur

said, 'Goodness is deeper than the deepest evil. However radical evil may be, it is not as deep as goodness.'

Yes, God enables us to make our way forward with a spark of goodness in the depths of our soul, a spark which asks only to burst into flame.

My mother remains for me a witness to joy and kind-heartedness. Already as a child she learned to be kind to everyone. In her family it was out of the question to demean others by words that ridiculed or judged them harshly.

She had complete confidence in her own children. Throughout our life, even if trials lead us to question ourselves, to discover our limits, that irreplaceable gift remains: 'You can have confidence in yourself.' That was what my mother wanted to communicate to each of her nine children.

She radiated great peace and that came from the troubles she had gone through. If she learned that something difficult had occurred, she would wait a few moments for calm to return, and then speak of something else, quite simply, as if nothing had happened. There was nothing fanatical about her, but she had a deep-seated joy. She seemed to conserve a kind of fullness of peace. And yet sometimes she told me, 'You think I am always at peace within, but in fact there is a deep struggle.'

A festival without end

The call to inner joy sets before us a fundamental choice: will we make the decision to live in the spirit of praise? During his life on earth, Christ sometimes prayed with tears and pleading, but also with a heart filled with joy.

Are we aware to what extent simple gestures can renew

joy? One day, from Latin America where he was living above all with the poor, our brother Robert, who was a physician and who is now deceased, sent me a short telegram for my birthday: 'May your festival have no end!'

Robert was referring to the thought of a believer of the fourth century, Saint Athanasius, that we had read together: 'The Risen Christ makes human life a continual festival.'

Yes, the wonder of a joy! The Gospel bears within it such a bright hope that we would like to go even to the point of giving ourselves in order to communicate it.

Where is the source of hope and of joy? It is in God, who tirelessly seeks us out and who finds in us the profound beauty of the human soul.

God makes us into poor people of the Gospel. He calls us to place our trust in him, in great simplicity. He keeps us close to him, beings who are crystal-clear, transparent as the springtime sky.

'Christ is light for every human being in the world.'[10] Will we be bearers of a Gospel light?

Jesus our peace, taking our burdens upon yourself, you enable us to wait until God's joy comes to touch the depths of our soul.

Happy the Simple-Hearted!

Simplicity of heart and of life

One of the first things Christ says in the Gospel is this: 'Happy the simple-hearted!'[11] Yes, happy those who head towards simplicity, simplicity of heart and simplicity of life.

A simple heart strives to live in the present moment, to welcome each day as God's today.

Does not the spirit of simplicity shine out in serene joy, and even in cheerfulness?

Simplifying our life enables us to share with the least fortunate, in order to alleviate suffering where there is disease, poverty, famine …

Our brothers in Taizé, as well as those living on other continents among the very poor, are keenly aware that we are called to a simple life. We have discovered that it does not keep us from offering hospitality day after day.

A surge of trusting

A simple heart does not claim to understand everything about faith on its own. It says to itself, 'Others understand better what I have trouble grasping and they help me to keep going.'

A Path of Hope

We live at a time when many people are asking: what is faith? Faith is a simple trust in God, an indispensable surge of trusting undertaken countless times over in the course of our life.

All of us can have doubts. They are nothing to worry about. Our deepest desire is to listen to Christ who whispers in our hearts, 'Do you have hesitations? Don't worry; even if your faith may be weak, the Holy Spirit remains with you always.'

Some, to their surprise, have made this discovery: God's love can come to fulfilment even in a soul touched by doubts.

Our personal prayer is also simple. Do we think that many words are needed in order to pray? No. It can happen that a few words, even inept ones, are enough to entrust everything to God, our fears as well as our hopes.

By surrendering ourselves to the Holy Spirit, we will find the way that leads from worry to confident trust. And we tell him:

> 'Holy Spirit, enable us
> to turn to you at every moment.
> So often we forget that you dwell in us,
> that you pray in us, that you love in us.
> Your presence in us is trust
> and constant forgiveness.'

Prayer does not make us less involved in the world. On the contrary, nothing is more responsible than to pray. The more we pray, humbly, the more we are led to love and to express it with our life.

At the wellsprings of trust

Where is the source of trusting? It is in God, who always offers us both his forgiveness and his presence.

By forgiving us, God removes what has wounded us, sometimes since childhood. Welcoming God's forgiveness enables us not to be racked by the memory – the sometimes distant memory – of certain events.

Could there be chasms of the unknown in us, sometimes an abyss of guilt coming from who knows where? God never threatens anyone and the forgiveness with which he inundates our lives brings healing to our soul. How could a God of love impose himself by threats? God is not a tyrant.

God also offers his constant presence. Even if we thought he were absent from our life, he loves us none the less for that.

And so we say to God and we can sing, 'You love us; your forgiveness and your presence bring the brightness of praise to birth in us.'

The eyes of the innocent

In a world where we are troubled by the incomprehensible suffering of the innocent, who would not wish to try and make the consolation of the Holy Spirit accessible through his or her own life?

The eyes of the innocent question us: how can we share hope with those who have lost even the desire to discover it?

Some of my brothers and I have occasionally spent time in a place of dire poverty. And links of deep trust are created with those in need.

We have vivid memories of Madras, in India. We spent some time living in a two-roomed dwelling in a district like many others in that city – open drains, mosquitoes, shacks some of whose roofs had been swept off by a storm the day before we arrived.

When the rain stopped, we visited our neighbours. Most of them were Hindus. They lived in what could hardly even be called huts. They were straw roofs that were very low, for protection against the rain and the sun. You had to stoop down to enter.

Going from shack to shack, we came upon a widow whose dwelling had been demolished; the wall that separated her from her neighbours had fallen and so the families could see one another.

In one of these huts, sheltered by the bit of roof remaining, a young father of eight children was stretched out. He was lying on a mat; the family did not own a blanket. He had asthma, and possibly tuberculosis. The dignity of that family was impressive.

We stayed there for several weeks. At the end of December, we left each day to join the thousands of young adults who had gathered for the meeting that my brothers had been preparing for two years.

Together with a number of local children we would get into a small rickshaw. And we came to an enormous 'church' that had been erected in just a few days, made of bamboo and matted coconut leaves. It was splendidly decorated, with oil lamps and garlands of flowers. In that temporary 'church' we all prayed together each day. The songs, particularly the age-old refrains of the Indian tradition, sustained by the beauty of human voices, expressed a contemplative waiting on God.

The participants had come from all the regions of India, from twenty Asian countries and from many countries of Europe. We were welcomed by the poor and the meeting took place in great simplicity. That was enough to fill our hearts to overflowing.

After the meeting, it was not easy to leave our neighbours in the district. Some of them had become like members of our family. The expressions on their faces were poignant. It was hard for them to see us leave. Their trust was like fire.

The sign of forgiveness

Another year, two of my brothers and I went to South Africa, at a time when racial tensions were strong and what was called apartheid was in force.

After a few days in Johannesburg we had been invited to Cape Town. At Crossroads, a black district where we had expected to meet only a few friends, a crowd had gathered for a prayer service. They were singing and the human voices conveyed a plea that came from the depths. African Church leaders asked me to speak.

I alluded to a man of God from South Africa whom my parents met when I was about five years old. My mother asked him to bless each of her children – my elder brother, my seven sisters and then me, the youngest. From that day on, I often heard my mother say, 'Faith is disappearing in Europe, but Africans will come to restore the Gospel to us in its pristine freshness.' I assured my listeners that that blessing of long ago was being fulfilled.

Then I tried to express by a symbolic gesture what filled my heart by saying, 'I would like to ask forgiveness of you, not in the name of the Whites, I could not do that, but because you are suffering for the Gospel. Would it be possible for me to go from one to the other so that each person could make the sign of the cross, the sign of Christ's forgiveness, in my hand?'

That sign was so well understood that everyone took part, the children as well as the older people. Songs of resurrection burst out spontaneously. But then men who were in charge of keeping an eye on the district arrived on big motorcycles, and we all had to leave.

The poor of the Gospel

Happy the simple-hearted! Yes, joy for those who aspire to head towards simplicity of heart and of life.

But simplifying never means choosing a harsh arrogance and a judgemental attitude towards those who have not taken the same road. The spirit of simplicity shines out in openness and in kind-heartedness. The simple-hearted are gentle; they remain poor people of the Gospel. Simplicity is nothing without charity.

Those who try to live in simplicity are concerned not to be 'masters of worry' but to remain 'servants of trust'. And today the human family has such a great need to enter into a time of trust and of comprehension.

God of consolation, we are sometimes troubled by the incomprehensible suffering of the innocent. Inspire all those who are seeking solutions so that hope may shine forth in the human family.

The Simplicity of a Child's Heart

Children and those like them

In a world where light and darkness co-exist, there are men, women, young people and children who are bearers of light. Their radiance is seen by others, even if they themselves are unaware of it.

Who can express adequately what some children can communicate by their simplicity, by their trust, by some unexpected words?

A little boy of nine confided to me: 'My father left us. I never see him, but I still love him and at night I pray for him.' That child was living the forgiveness of the Gospel. Was he not a pure reflection of God's goodness?

One day Christ said, 'Let the little children come to me; the realities of God belong to those who are like them.'[12] Did he want to make us attentive to welcome the Gospel in that part of ourselves where the spirit of our childhood remains?

Sometimes adults feel they acquire authority by taking a serious or even a pessimistic view of things. Vigilance is necessary if we are not to let ourselves be paralysed by those who dramatize situations and can foster fear. Gloom is more contagious than joy and peace of heart.

What does it mean for someone who is fully an adult to

combine the spirit of childhood and the maturity that comes from long years of experience?

Though childhood has no monopoly on trust, God makes himself accessible to the humble hearts that surrender themselves to him.

There is nothing naïve about deep-seated trust; it goes hand in hand with discernment. A childlike spirit is clear-sighted candour. Far from being simplistic, it is lucid as well. The positive elements in a situation, as well as the negative ones, are both present to it.

The spirit of childhood is wonder. Drawn from the Gospel, it is sometimes like the secret of an intimate joy.

When I am with young people, I sometimes think, 'You were not made to speak in public. Nothing prepared you for it; it came too late in life for you.' And then I say to myself, 'Speak with the simplicity of a child's heart. Are you so different today than you were when your oldest sister taught you to read and write?'

When I was a child, I lived with my parents, my brother and my seven sisters in a mountain village, as poor as one can imagine. I was the youngest. At the age of 6 or 7, I was struck by the poverty of some of the inhabitants. In particular there was one old woman whom one of my sisters and I helped to move house. We then discovered that, except for her bed, all that she owned could fit into a baby carriage that we pulled from one house to the other, along a steep road.

During the Advent season I would buy little presents in the tiny shop in the village. I brought them home, wrapped them and hid them under my bed, waiting for Christmas to come so I could distribute them to the poorest families.

When the joy of giving is awakened in a child's heart, it remains for life. Still today there are three drawers under my bed filled with little gifts that I like to give to those who come to see me, especially children.

Wounded innocence

One Sunday in the autumn of 1983, Mother Teresa came to Taizé. With her, during prayer, we expressed a concern: 'In Calcutta there are visible homes for the dying but, in many parts of the world, many young people seem to be living in invisible homes for the dying. A subtle doubt is fostered in them by broken relationships that touch them to the quick.'

Yes, in the Western world some young people are marked by broken relationships or family tensions. When as children they have seen members of their family quarrel or even separate, their hearts are often torn apart. They can feel rejected, and in them is born an inner appeal not to be abandoned.

How can the wounded heart of a child be healed? Understanding someone very young requires discretion and tact. Sometimes the question comes to mind: what has happened to this child? Could he or she have been humiliated at school, on the street, or perhaps at home? Will someone be there to listen to them and remain alongside them with infinite discretion?

On a visit to my brothers who have been sharing the life of the poor in Bangladesh for the last thirty years, I saw, in a narrow alley, a child squatting on the ground, taking a baby in one arm and trying to pick up a second one with his other arm. When he managed to lift them both, he fell over. Then these words came to my mind, which I heard on the day the Second Vatican Council ended: 'Human beings are sacred by the wounded innocence of their childhood.'[13]

'Whatever you do for the least ...'

Speaking of Mother Teresa, I would like to say that I had many opportunities to converse with her over the years. Often it was possible to discern in her reflections of the holiness of Christ.

She came to Taizé for the first time in 1976. Our hill was packed with young people from many different countries. Together we wrote a prayer: 'O God, Father of every human being, you ask us all to bring love where the poor are humiliated, reconciliation where human beings are divided, joy where the Church is shaken. You open this road for us so that we may be ferments of communion throughout the entire human family.'

That same year, a few of my brothers and I went to live for a time with the very poor in Calcutta. We were staying near her home in a noisy lower-class district. Children could be seen everywhere. We were offered hospitality by a Christian family whose home was in front of an intersection of some small streets, with shops and simple workshops.

Mother Teresa often came to pray with us. She brought us a wooden tabernacle; she wanted us to have the Eucharist reserved in our small chapel. She knew that it is an essential wellspring to sustain the gift of one's entire life.

That woman of God had energies of rare intensity and she took spontaneous initiatives. One day, while we were returning from a visit to some people with leprosy, she said to me in the car, 'I have something to ask you. Say yes!' Before giving an answer, I tried to learn more about what she wanted, but she would only repeat, 'Say yes!' Finally she explained, 'Tell me that from now on you will wear your white robe all day long; this sign is necessary in the situations of our time.' 'Yes,' I answered, 'I will speak to my brothers and I will wear it as often as I can.' So she had her sisters make a white robe for me and she insisted on sewing part of it herself.

Mother Teresa proposed that I go to the home for abandoned children each morning with one of my brothers, who was a doctor, to take care of those who were most ill. From the first day I got to know a little girl, four months old. I was told that she was in danger of not surviving, that she did not have enough strength to resist the winter viruses. And Mother Teresa proposed, 'Bring her with you to Taizé; you will be able to take care of her there.'

In the plane returning to France, the child was not well. She threw up almost everything we gave her to eat. The first weeks, she often slept in my arms while I worked.

Slowly her strength returned and she began to be restored to health. Then she went to live in the village, in a house close to ours. My sister Genevieve, who many years before in Taizé had taken in children and raised them as her own, welcomed her to her home. That child, named Marie, grew up with Genevieve and called her 'grandmother'. I was her godfather when she was baptized and I love her like a father.

Very quickly the child showed her exuberant nature. When I came to see her in the morning she would jump for joy and run around. One evening, when she was four years old, she was with me while I was having supper with a rather distinguished visitor. While he and

I were speaking, she was under the table undoing his shoelaces.

At that time, we used to go for a few minutes each morning to church to pray. Already she grasped something of the mystery of God. Does not what a human being has discovered as a child remain throughout his or her lifetime?

At the age of six, Marie went through a trial, the unexpected illness of someone close to her. My brothers and I were leaving for Rome where we were going to spend two or three weeks. Marie made me understand that she wished to come with us. In Rome we met Pope John Paul II several times. At the end of our stay Marie said to me, 'The Pope kissed me six times!'

During those days in Rome, Marie could not leave me. She needed me to hold her hand and for us always to be together. Late one evening I had to leave for a meeting. She realized this, woke up and insisted on getting up and coming with me.

Mother Teresa and I were invited to the opening of the first World Youth Day in Rome. We were asked to speak in the Colosseum, one after the other. Little Marie, who was eight years old, was there too. The wind was blowing so strongly that I had to hold her tightly wrapped in her cape so that she would not be pierced by the cold. With her keen and attentive mind, she tried to listen to everything.

Later on, we were invited once again to lead a prayer for World Youth Day, this time in Denver, in the United States. But Mother Teresa was already ill. When I arrived, I learned that she had had to cancel her trip. She sent me a letter telling me: 'Let's write a fourth book together!'

I learned of Mother Teresa's death in utterly

unexpected circumstances. Marie had left with my sister for a short holiday in the mountains. Marie called me and insisted that I come and join them, if only for a short time. It was there that we heard the news. Then I understood why I had gone to that place. It was not without importance that we were together that evening.

The following week, two of my brothers and I went to Calcutta in order to take part in the funeral. We wished to thank God for Mother Teresa's gift of her life and to sing with her sisters in the spirit of praise.

Next to her body, I remembered that we had one conviction in common: a communion in God stimulates us to alleviate human suffering on earth. Yes, when we soothe the trials of others, we encounter Christ. Does he not say it himself: 'Whatever you do for the least, you do for me, Christ.'[14]

Awakening others to the mystery of trust

Who will find ways of awakening children and young people to the mystery of trust in God? An intuition, already glimpsed in a person's early years, even if it is later forgotten, can reappear throughout their life.

When this awakening to faith happens at home, children acquire an irreplaceable gift. Today, in secularized societies, it is good to have a few symbols in our homes that give glimpses of an invisible presence. A corner for prayer can be set up, with an icon lit by a candle. Happy are those who, at a very young age, have been made attentive by their families to a communion in God!

To communicate this trust to a child, many words are not needed. It is already something to place one's hand on his or her forehead at night while saying 'God is love'[15] or 'the peace of Christ' ...

So many elderly people think they have accomplished nothing; they are forced to end their lives in loneliness. And yet some of them, abounding in selflessness, are indispensable for the younger generations. They listen, and in this way free others from burdensome worries. More spiritual mothers and fathers according to the Gospel exist than we think.

When I arrived in Taizé in 1940, the welcome of a few old women in the village touched me. One of them was called Marie Auboeuf. The mother of several children, she had a deep faith. She told me that, many years before my arrival, when her children were still little, she had suffered greatly from a progressive paralysis of the hip. There was no electricity in the house, but one night the room where she was sleeping was filled with light. When she got up, her paralysis was less acute.

When I came to know Marie Auboeuf, the World War was in progress. I was still alone. From where did she draw the intuition that enabled her to understand the desire that filled me and the vocation I was preparing to live? That elderly woman was an image of unexpected serenity.

Jesus our hope, turn us into humble people of the Gospel. We so deeply desire to understand that in us the best is built up through simple trust ... and even a child can manage this.

A Life of Communion in God

The desire for God

As far back as we look in history, multitudes of believers have known that, through prayer, God brings a light within.

Already before Christ, a believer expressed a yearning: 'My soul longs for you in the night, Lord; my spirit within me is seeking you.'[16]

Three centuries after Christ, Saint Augustine wrote, 'A desire that calls out to God is already a prayer. If you want to pray ceaselessly, then never stop desiring …'[17]

The desire for communion with God has been set within the human heart since the dawn of time. The mystery of that communion touches what is most intimate in us, the very depths of our being.

And so we can say to Christ, 'To whom would we go but to you? You have the words that bring our soul back to life.'[18]

God's presence remains invisible

'God is Spirit'[19] and his presence remains invisible. He lives within us always, in times of darkness as well as when everything is bathed in light.

29

Dwelling in the centre of each person's soul, God does not necessarily communicate with us by means of human words. God speaks above all by silent intuitions.

Remaining in God's presence in a peaceful silence is already praying. And at times a simple sigh can be a prayer.

This silence seems like nothing. And yet through it the Holy Spirit can enable us to welcome God's joy.

Could the impression arise that God is far away, as if for a fleeting moment the inward eye could no longer see? We should remember that God never withdraws his presence. We can entrust everything to him, lay down everything in him.

When we pray and nothing seems to happen, does our prayer remain unanswered? No. In quiet trust in God, all prayer finds some kind of fulfilment. Perhaps it is different from what we expected ... Does not God answer us with a view to a greater love?

When we sense hardly anything of God's presence, what good is there in agonizing over it?

It is enough to have the simple desire to welcome God's love for a flame to be kindled. Animated by the Holy Spirit, this flame of love is perhaps very frail. And yet it burns.

And the Holy Spirit stirs us up and is at work within us, reorientating the depths of our being.

The Holy Spirit never leaves our soul: even at death communion with God remains. Knowing that God welcomes us forever into his love becomes a source of confidence.

In my room there is a photo of my great-grandmother. She had lost her husband and three sons to tuberculosis. Her grandson, my uncle, was not a believer. When he realized she was dying, he said to her, 'You have gone through so much. I have no faith; can you tell me something?' He was twenty years old then. She made no reply. A week later, he came back to see her. 'What I see is beautiful,' she told him. And she died.

Praying with almost nothing

One day a long time ago I spent a few moments in our pottery workshop. The brothers working there used to write a few words on a blackboard. That day there were these words: 'Your love, O Christ, has wounded my soul. I go forward singing your praises.'

Were they the authors of such a profound thought? No, they said; it was written in the seventh century by John Climacus in his old age. At the age of fifteen, he had entered the monastery of Sinai. He had realized that God's love is expressed through a person's whole being – body, flesh and spirit.

Sometimes, it is true that we pray with almost nothing. We can feel as if we had been stripped bare. Happy is the one who can then say to Christ: 'Christ Jesus, I hide nothing in my heart from you. You know how hard it is for me to express my desire for communion with you. You yourself shared the human condition. You know that I am sometimes pulled in different directions at the same time. But when my inner being experiences a void, a thirst for your presence remains within me. And when I am unable to pray, you yourself are my prayer.'

Christ too surrendered himself to God. When he died on the cross, he prayed: 'Into your hands I commit my spirit',[20] in other words, 'I entrust my entire life to you.'

During my adolescence, when I was recovering from tuberculosis, I used to take long walks. There were moments when a premonition passed through my mind like lightning: one day, I would have to take great risks for Christ and the Gospel. I would have to walk along a road I was still far from recognizing.

I realized then that, in order to go forward with confidence, it was essential to root my life in a few simple Gospel realities to which I could constantly return.

During those long walks, I used to repeat these words: 'Love solitude and hate isolation.' Then some other words came to the fore: 'Abandon yourself to him'; 'In all things inner silence, peace of heart'; 'Live in joy, simplicity and mercy'.

Today I would still say as I used to: whoever attempts to surrender themselves to the Holy Spirit has to allow themselves to be built up inwardly by means of a few intuitions from the Gospel, sometimes discovered early in life. They can become a kind of rock on which to rely.

Not a great many words but just a few, succinct and clear. Do we sometimes forget them for a while? They can be taken up again at the very moment when they reappear.

The simple beauty of prayer with others

The vocation of our community has always included two aspirations: to go forward in an inner life through prayer, and to take on responsibilities to make the earth a better place to live. The two cannot be separated.

Could the Gospel be calling us to bring together in our life the gifts of a creator with two feet planted firmly on the ground and the thirst of a mystical soul?

All who walk in the steps of Christ hold themselves in the presence of God while remaining alongside other people as well. Prayer is a serene force at work within human beings, never allowing them to doze off. From it we draw indispensable energies of compassion.

If some people find it hard to pray alone, the beauty of a sung prayer, even with just two or three people together, is an incomparable support for the inner life. Through simple words as well as singing that goes on and on, it can radiate joy. A sung prayer with others allows the desire for God to well up in us and helps us enter into contemplative waiting.

Yes, let our hearts rejoice! The simple beauty of prayer with others is one of the places where the spirit of praise is renewed. Is not sung prayer one of the first gifts of our resurrection?

And surprisingly, at a time when, in vast regions of the world, faith is ebbing away, the Holy Spirit is transmitted chiefly through common prayer.

Already in the early years of our community, my brothers and I used to sing. We were able to sing chorales of rare beauty in four-part harmony. I understood then that singing was an irreplaceable support for community prayer.

Why have singing and music always been so important in Taizé? I think that it goes back to my childhood. My mother had undertaken advanced voice training at the Paris Conservatory. Under the direction of the composer Vincent d'Indy, she gave solo performances at concerts. Later on, while having to take care of the daily needs of her children, she continued to practise her singing every day. Her intimate desire was that this should be a way for her soul to open up. From her singing she drew great serenity. As a child, I often heard her singing in the evening when I was in my room, leaving the door ajar.

One of my mother's aunts, Caroline Delachaux, went

to study the piano for four years in Germany, at Weimar. She passed the virtuoso examination with her teacher, Hans von Bülow, in the presence of Franz Liszt. A very cheerful woman, she taught my sisters music. There were three pianos in the house and several of my sisters played.

Genevieve, the youngest, was exceptionally talented. While she was preparing her own virtuoso examination in Lausanne, some children who had lost their parents in the war were brought to us in Taizé. I asked Genevieve to come to take charge of them for a limited time.

At first there were three children, but soon there were twenty of them. Genevieve decided to devote her life to them. Although she was an artist with her whole being, she gave up all thought of a musical career and had her piano brought to Taizé.

When she was quite elderly, Genevieve had a fall. Her hands suffered from it and for some time she could no longer play. To encourage her to begin again, we bought a keyboard, put it next to the old piano, and someone would play along with her. Gradually she began again and today she still plays as often as she can.

Nothing is more responsible than to pray

Throughout the year 1981 the situation in Poland was difficult. In May, Cardinal Wyszynski was seriously ill in Warsaw. That same month, the Polish pope John Paul II was the victim of an attempt on his life that brought him close to death and that forced him to undergo two long periods in hospital. In December, martial law was going to be decreed in the country.

That year, invited for the fourth time to speak at the yearly pilgrimage of mineworkers in Silesia, I arrived one

A Glimmer of Happiness

May evening with another brother at Warsaw airport. There were young people waiting for us; from a distance we heard the songs of Taizé being sung.

Why this deep sympathy for the young people of Poland? Perhaps because we have discovered that in the Polish soul there is little pretentiousness but a humble trust in God. That trust has given the Christians of that country the ability to remain faithful, to endure, to persevere in spite of trials.

At the airport the young people told us that the cardinal had just died. We were brought at once to the place where his body was lying in state. Seeing that enormous crowd, stiff with sorrow, passing in front of him made it clear just what that man of God represented. With courage, he had never given in; he was the symbol of Polish resistance.

In Krakow we found again the places where, several years earlier, the future John Paul II had received us so warmly. There, as everywhere else, we heard the same preoccupation: if the pope were to die following the attempt on his life, it would be the end of hope in Poland.

At Katowice a small group of our brothers was waiting for us. They had been preparing a meeting of young people for some time already. They were living simply and didn't look too well; there was not much to eat then in the country.

What struck us about the meeting of young people, compared to previous years, was the great stride forward. Everything was very intense. Saturday evening, in a packed church, we celebrated a prayer that went on until very late at night. Together with the young people we asked ourselves: what can we do so that commitment for others does not cause us to forget the wellsprings of faith and prayer?

A Path of Hope

On Sunday, the pilgrimage of the mineworkers took place in Piekary. There had never been so many of them: I was told that 200,000 men were present. From the top of the hill, you could see a human ocean. The bishop had no qualms about speaking out strongly, just as the future pope used to do when he led the pilgrimage. He was incredibly courageous and surprisingly open. Thunderous applause punctuated his words on freedom.

This kind of pilgrimage of men is unique in the world and the friendship shown to us was exceedingly beautiful. I was asked to give a meditation. I spoke about prayer, which continues at the heart of human activities. Nothing is more responsible than to pray: it is possible to have a constant inner reference to God while making a valiant commitment to work for freedom.

At the end of my talk I said to them, 'Tomorrow morning I will go to Rome. I will bring the pope, in his hospital room, a bouquet of wild flowers from Poland. I will tell him that all together we are attempting to be bearers of reconciliation, not only among Christians but also in the divisions that tear apart the human family.'

After the pilgrimage we had to leave immediately for Warsaw, to attend the funeral of Cardinal Wyszynski. We did manage to see briefly the young people from other Eastern European countries, who had come to take part discreetly in our meeting.

The next morning we took the flight for Italy, bringing the flowers we had picked that morning, a simple bouquet of buttercups. In Rome we learned that the pope's situation had worsened. Would it be possible to visit him? At the clinic Father Stanislaus, his secretary, welcomed us. He told me that I would be able to see the Holy Father but that the brother with me could not enter the room.

As soon as I went in, John Paul II held out his arms and embraced me. Lying in bed, he was pale and overcome with emotion. If I had known he was in such a weakened state, I would not have dared to call from Poland asking to come. The buttercups were on his knees. I spoke a few words to him about his country; he listened attentively. Then he pronounced words coming from a man who had reflected a great deal about death. He concluded by saying, 'Continue! Go on!'

On leaving him, I said to myself that the ministry of a pope could sometimes come close to an invisible martyrdom because of Christ and the Gospel.

When our lips are closed

Unchanging in its essence, prayer can take on a diversity of expressions. Some people pray in a great silence. Remaining in silence in the presence of God, with the desire to welcome his Holy Spirit, is already seeking him.

There are those who express themselves with many words. Saint Teresa of Avila wrote, 'When I speak to the Lord, often I do not know what I am saying.'

Others pray with just a few words. Spoken slowly or sung, five or ten times, from the bottom of the heart, these words can sustain a life of communion in God. For example these short prayers: 'All God can do is give his love, our God is tenderness'; 'My soul rests in peace in God alone.'

When we pray, we try to express what is most personal in us. Sometimes, an inspiration or an intuition wells up from the depths of our being. But there is no need to worry if no words arise. There can be resistances and blind spots in us, times when in prayer our lips remain shut.

At that point Saint Augustine reminds us: 'There is also a voice of the heart and a language of the heart ... That inner voice is our prayer when our lips are closed and our soul open before God. We remain silent and our heart speaks, not to human ears but to God. Be sure that God will listen to you.'[21]

> *Holy Spirit, you always come to us and, in us, there is wonder at a presence. Our prayer may be quite poor, but you pray even in the silence of our hearts.*

Mystery of Communion

'Communion', one of the most beautiful
names of the Church

If we could always remember that Christ is communion . . .

He did not come to earth to start one more religion, but to offer to all a communion in God. His disciples are called to be a humble leaven of trust and peace within humanity.

When communion among Christians is a life and not a theory, it radiates hope. Still more, it can help sustain the indispensable search for world peace.

How, then, could Christians still remain divided?

Reconciliation among Christians is urgent today; it cannot continually be put off until later, until the end of time.

Over the years, the ecumenical vocation has fostered an invaluable exchange of views. This dialogue is the first fruit of reconciliation. But when the ecumenical vocation is not made concrete through a communion, it leads nowhere.

In Damascus, there lives the Greek Orthodox Patriarch of Antioch, Ignatius IV. He wrote these striking words: 'Our divisions make Christ unrecognizable. We have an urgent need for prophetic initiatives in order to bring ecumenism out of the twists and turns in which I fear it is getting stuck. We have an urgent need for prophets and saints to help our Churches to be converted by mutual forgiveness.' And the patriarch called for 'emphasizing the language of communion rather than that of jurisdiction.'[22]

Pope John Paul II, while receiving in Rome leaders of the Orthodox Church of Greece, spoke of 'the ecumenism of holiness which will lead us finally towards full communion, which is neither absorption or fusion, but an encounter in truth and love.'[23]

In the long history of Christians, multitudes discovered one day that they were divided, sometimes without even knowing why. Today it is essential to do everything in our power so that as many Christians as possible – who are often innocent of the divisions – may discover that they are in communion.

Could the Church give signs of great openness, so wide as to let it become clear that those who used to be divided in the past are no longer separated, but are already living in communion?

A significant step will have been accomplished to the extent that a life of communion, already a reality in certain places throughout the world, is explicitly taken into account. It will require courage to recognize this and draw the necessary conclusions. Written documents will come later. Does not putting the accent on written documents cause us in the end to lose sight of the Gospel's call to be reconciled without delay?[24]

Vast numbers of people have a desire for reconciliation that touches the very depths of their soul. They aspire to this infinite joy: one love, one heart, one and the same communion.

Yes, communion is the touchstone. It comes to birth first of all in the heart of hearts of every Christian, in silence and in love. It begins in the present moment, within each person.

There are Christians who, without waiting, are already in communion with one another in the places where they live, quite humbly, quite simply.

Through their own life, they would like to make Christ present for many others. They know that the Church does not exist for itself but for the world, to place within it a ferment of peace.

'Communion' is one of the most beautiful names of the Church. In it there can be no severity towards one another, but only transparency, heartfelt kindness, compassion ...

In that unique communion which is the Church, God offers us all we need in order to go to the wellsprings: the Gospel, the Eucharist, the peace of forgiveness ... And Christ's holiness is no longer something unattainable; it is there, close at hand.

Can I recall here that my maternal grandmother discovered intuitively a kind of key to the ecumenical vocation, and that she opened a way which I then tried to put into practice? After the First World War, her deepest desire was that no one should ever have to go through what she had gone through. Since Christians had been waging war against each other in Europe, she thought, let them at least be reconciled, in order to prevent another war. She came from an old Protestant family but, living out an inner reconciliation, she began to go to the Catholic Church, without at the same time making any break with her own people.

Impressed by the testimony of her life, when I was still fairly young I found my own Christian identity by reconciling within myself the faith of my origins with the mystery of the Catholic faith, without breaking fellowship with anyone.[25]

A Path of Hope

> *'We will not try to find out who was*
> *wrong or right'*

In the early years of our community there was a cardinal in Lyons by the name of Pierre Gerlier. He was one of the first Church leaders to show confidence in us. He soon became a kind of spiritual father for us.

It was he who took the initiative in 1958 to introduce us to John XXIII, immediately after his election as pope. Wishing to place in his heart the question of the reconciliation of Christians, the cardinal asked John XXIII to receive Taizé at one of his first audiences. Why so quickly? The pope was elderly, the cardinal explained, and very soon he would hear a great many words, so it was important that he should remember well what we would tell him.

John XXIII accepted 'provided that they don't ask questions that are too difficult'. And so he received us immediately after the inauguration of his ministry, on the first morning when private audiences were held. His welcome was very simple, full of spontaneity. When we spoke to him of reconciliation, the pope clapped his hands and said, 'Bravo! Bravo!' He asked us to come back so we could continue our conversation.

That day was a kind of beginning for our community. John XXIII transmitted to us a kind of unexpected surge of life and marked us with an irreplaceable imprint. By his life, that beloved pope opened our eyes to the ministry of a universal pastor, so essential at the heart of that unique communion which is the Church.

The enormous pastoral responsibility entrusted to him in his old age certainly brought to fruition in him an exceptional intuition regarding communion among Christians. He placed that intuition in the awareness of many.

Announcing a council in 1959, John XXIII pronounced words that are among the most crystal-clear imaginable. Here are those words of light: 'We will not try to find out who was wrong, we will not try to find out who was right, we will only say: Let us be reconciled!'[26]

For the Church no one is a stranger, no one is excluded, no one is far away

Ten years earlier, in 1949, the same Cardinal Gerlier had already suggested that we go to Rome to make ecumenical contacts, though at the time almost nobody had heard of the name of Taizé. He had asked an Italian prelate, Giovanni Battista Montini, to welcome us. Immediately a relationship of profound confidence began with him, a man of openness and of prayer, and that relationship continued throughout the following years.

In 1963, Giovanni Battista Montini was elected to succeed the beloved John XXIII; he became pope and took the name of Paul VI. From then on he received us each year in a private audience. I would like to relate something about this pope, sometimes a bit forgotten between the two ministries of John XXIII and John Paul II, which were so exceptional.

Pope Paul VI knew how to find symbolic gestures to express his humanity. During the Second Vatican Council, to which we had been invited, he was aware that twice a day my brothers and I used to receive bishops at table in our flat in Rome. One evening, someone from the Vatican arrived with a crate of apples and a crate of pears that the pope had received and wished to share with us.

Paul VI liked to give us presents. I was embarrassed

because we never accept gifts. Once I said to him, 'We will give this present to someone else.' But Paul VI insisted, 'No, it's for Taizé.' How could we say no? The most beautiful thing we have from him is a chalice, for the celebration of the Eucharist. We keep it together with John XXIII's breviary, which his secretary gave us after his death.

Paul VI was the first pope to undertake long trips across the continents. In 1968, he invited me to go with him to Colombia, in the same plane. At Bogotá our brother Robert and I stayed in a *favela*, a very poor district on the edge of the city.

Paul VI had so much confidence in us that he wished to set up a closer relationship with our little community. In July 1971 he sent someone from Rome to see us in Taizé, with whom a simple letter was signed. That letter stated that henceforth there would be a 'representative of the prior of Taizé to the Holy See,' so that there could be a direct link. That link still continues today.

Several weeks later, when I received a telephone call saying that the news was going to be made public by the official newspaper of the Vatican, I went out alone to walk in the garden. The night's heavy rain was steaming up, warmed by the sun-gorged earth. When I returned, I wrote the following lines in my journal:

'Who are you in this event? I see myself, a poor man walking on the wild grass. I still cannot assess the extent of this agreement signed three weeks ago. But one thing I do know: I love that "pilgrim Church that is at Rome" and its bishop. What can I ask of him? Surely to give us light, to foster communion among all who refer to Christ?'

In December 1971, at the close of a conversation with Paul VI, I said some words I had not intended to speak:

'The name of Taizé is sometimes heavy for us to bear.' 'The name of Taizé cannot vanish,' replied the pope. And he made a generous parallel with another historical place. Paul VI went on to add: 'The first time that we met, you told me that you were pilgrims. I have always remembered that.' Yes, we are pilgrims; our means are poor. And the Pope concluded, 'I too am poor.'

Paul VI was anxious to support pastoral involvement with the younger generations and he was attentive to our experience. In December 1972, our audience had been fixed for eight o'clock in the evening. Paul VI had carefully read the report in which I had tried to express certain characteristic trends of present-day consciousness. My question was how, instead of rejecting these trends, could we take them on board?

After our conversation, we went to the pope's private chapel for a simple prayer and a moment of silence. 'I know how fond you are of silence at Taizé,' the pope said. Then our conversation continued over the meal. My heart was full on finding Paul VI so able to understand the way young people think.

As we parted, I was walking beside him in the corridor of his apartment and he said to me, 'Brother Roger, if you have the key for understanding the young, tell me what it is.' 'I would like to have that key,' I answered, 'but I do not have it, and never shall. We have no method at Taizé to communicate the faith.'

A few years later, it was in May 1977, the pope listened with close attention and was interested in our experiences in Calcutta with young people from every continent. He said, 'I would not like to fail those young people who take their commitment so far.' Later: 'I would like to be worthy of them.' Then he asked, 'What can I do for them?' The older he grew the more his mystical side animated him. His candour was poignant. His reflection starting from his own life was so surprising that, looking at that man so devastated by trials, some words sprang spontaneously to my lips: 'In you there are marks of the holiness of Christ.'

On August 6, 1978 we were outdoors under the trees, just finishing the last prayer of the day when our brother Alain came and whispered in my ear: 'They just announced on the radio that Paul VI has died.' We knelt down again to pray.

Even in his old age Paul VI was still passionately concerned about the future of humanity. Every time I spoke to him about the young, he was all attention. He understood their searching. No warnings from him. He expressed his confidence in them. He had received reports on us and they were not always favourable, yet his confidence in us was unshaken.

Paul VI was a man of great courage. He had an equal ability both to analyse and to summarize a situation. He found himself confronted with a tempest, a deep crisis in the Church that went so far, it seemed to him, that 'his authority ended at the door of his office'. He spoke those very words to me one day. But through what he was, he opened the roads of the future with surprising sensitivity and exceptional intelligence. In that way he prepared what the beloved Pope John Paul II would accomplish after him.

Those who re-read what Paul VI wrote know that his texts are a goldmine of reflection, the full import of which will only appear later. For example, when he wrote, 'For the Church no one is a stranger, no one is excluded, no one is far away.'[27]

A Glimmer of Happiness

A long-expected event

In 1962, a year after the Berlin wall was built, our brother Christophe, who has since died, said to us, 'It would be so important for brothers of our community to go two by two to the countries of Eastern Europe and have meetings with young and old, to listen and try to understand.' He was German. As a young man, at the end of the Second World War, he had been taken to the Soviet Union as a prisoner of war and spent three years there.

We followed his intuition and, for decades, we were continually coming and going in the countries of Eastern Europe. He himself began with East Germany. It would not have been bearable to enjoy the great freedom of the West and to know that those we loved in the East were tormented by what they had to endure, without going often to be with them.

We did not talk about this. It was important to be discreet so as not to compromise those we were visiting. After the borders were opened, we continued these visits. And if we welcome so many East European young people to Taizé today, that is a result of those long years when trust was being established between us.

At the time when East Germany was so closed, among the friends that my brothers went unobtrusively to meet there were several Lutheran bishops. I have never forgotten the visit one of them made to Taizé. One day he had obtained a rare authorization to come with two other people. One of my brothers went to the railway station to meet them. As soon as they got out of the train, the bishop made a covert sign to him indicating that one of the three was there to listen and to report on everything that was said when they returned.

Despite that awkward presence, we managed to get to talk with the bishop alone. An excursion to visit Cluny was organized for the group, but he pretended to be ill, remained in Taizé and took advantage of those hours to come and see me in my room. During our last meal, he did not hesitate to utter courageous words about the situation in his country.

One of our most intimate friends was the Lutheran bishop of Dresden, Johannes Hempel. Beginning in 1974 he tried to invite me to his city for a meeting of young people but was unable to get permission for this. After a series of unsuccessful attempts, in 1980 he received with difficulty a lukewarm agreement from the authorities. Several of my brothers went quietly to Dresden ahead of time to lend their support to the preparations for the meeting. I arrived with some others with no visa, because Johannes Hempel had only received the necessary paper the day before the meeting. He was at the airport. Were we going to be denied entrance? Whether we would cross customs or not remained uncertain until the last minute.

That first meeting in East Germany was certainly the most impressive of all. In the evening, thousands of young people from different regions of East Germany were together in a large church, the 'Kreuzkirche,' for a prayer that lasted late into the night. To see the faces of young people whom we had loved for years without ever having known was a festival for the heart. They were packed in right to the back of the high galleries. Some 150 Czechs and Slovaks had been able to come. They were careful not to manifest their presence too openly, but they did come together for a few moments in a room so that we could meet them and pray with them.

In God's eternity our brother Christophe must certainly have shared the joy in what we had accomplished. He so much wanted contacts in East Germany to continue.

After the prayer, Johannes Hempel was so moved that he could no longer speak. He had just experienced something he had longed for for such a long time. Late at night, he brought me to his home, put on a record, and his family and I remained in silence for a long time, listening to the music.

His house was bugged. Before I left, he suggested that we take a short walk along the Elbe so that we could speak freely. That walk by the river will remain for ever in my memory. I felt that I could speak to him about what concerned us. He was so open-minded that I could tell him everything. Immediately afterwards, I noted down these words in my journal: 'Johannes Hempel: where could we find a man more attentive and unafraid, incomparably open?'

The joy of the Holy Spirit visible among us

In 1978 I was able to go for the first time to Moscow and St Petersburg, which was then known as Leningrad. Christians there were being sorely tested.

A new invitation arrived ten years later, for the thousand-year celebrations of Russia's baptism. The Orthodox Church offered a warm welcome: it was clear that our little community was loved. The day after we arrived, one of my brothers and I were brought into the council that brought together all the Russian bishops in the monastery of the Trinity-Saint Sergius. The singing was unequalled in its expressive force – a visitation from God, the joy of the Holy Spirit visible among us.

We had planned to spend four days there, but we

stayed almost two weeks. It was deeply touching to see among the humble people of Moscow, Yaroslavl and Kiev so many faces marked by peace and kindness. I said to myself, if we had come only to see those faces, reflections of God's holiness, by itself that would have been enough to fill our hearts to overflowing. So many maltreated Christians persevered and did not lose their faith, in spite of the enormous burden of fears. What a radiance it is that sustains that mystical people!

One day in Moscow I had a conversation with a young Russian translator. At one point she took a well-worn New Testament from her bag and said to me, 'My grandmother gave this to me.' 'What touched me the most in my grandmother's life,' she added, 'was her selflessness, the gift of herself. That made her faith in God credible.' Who will express adequately all that so many elderly women in Russia were able to communicate to the young in the course of those difficult years?

At the end of our stay some Orthodox Church leaders showed us one of the 5000 copies of the millennium Bible, which they had been allowed to print in Russian for the first time in seventy years. I told them that, twenty years earlier, at the end of the Second Vatican Council, some Latin American bishops told us how much they needed New Testaments. Our community had a million printed, to be distributed in all the dioceses of the continent, and it was the first New Testament translated into the Spanish of Latin America. A few years later, we likewise sent the bishops of Brazil half a million New Testaments in Portuguese. When they heard this the Russian bishops remarked, 'We would need not a million Bibles, but twenty million of them!'

Those words stayed with me in the days that followed. Back in Taizé, we thought about it and prayed. And my brothers and I decided we could run the risk of printing in France a million New Testaments in Russian, reproducing the millennium edition.

The Soviet regime was still in place. In February 1989, without having received any written authorization, nine lorries left France loaded with New Testaments in Russian. They were able to cross customs and arrived in Moscow, Minsk, Kiev and Leningrad. The costs of that edition were taken care of through the solidarity of West European Christians.

In Taizé we love the Orthodox Church with all our heart, with all our soul. In its places of worship, the beauty of the singing, the incense, the icons, windows open on the realities of God, the symbols and the gestures of the liturgy celebrated in the communion of Christians for centuries – everything invites one to discern 'heaven's joy on earth'. The being as a whole is affected, not just the mind, but the affectivity as well, and even the body itself.

How can we express enough gratitude to the Orthodox Christians of Russia, Belarus and Ukraine for what they have been in the trials they went through for seventy years, and for what they are today? How can we be adequately attentive to the gifts placed in the peoples of Romania, Serbia, Bulgaria and Greece?

O God, we praise you for the multitudes of women, men, young people and even children who, across the earth, are striving to be witnesses to peace, reconciliation and communion.

A Future of Peace

All God can do is love

Today more than ever before a call is arising to open paths of trust even in humanity's darkest hours. Can we hear that call?

There are people who, by giving themselves, attest that human beings are not doomed to hopelessness. Their perseverance enables them to look at the future with deep confidence. Through them do we not see signs of an undeniable hope arise, even in the most troubled situations of the world?

These people are mindful of the untold suffering of the innocent. They know all too well, in particular, that poverty in the world is on the rise, and that so many children are in distress.

They know that neither misfortunes nor the injustice of poverty come from God. All God can do is love. God looks at every human being with infinite tenderness and deep compassion.

When we realize that God loves even the most forsaken human being, then our hearts open to others. We are made more aware of the dignity of each person and we ask ourselves: how can we help prepare a different future?

Others can recognize our trust in God when we express it by the simple giving of ourselves for others. Faith becomes credible and is passed on above all when it is lived out.

'Love and say it with your life': these words were written three centuries after Christ by Saint Augustine.

Loving with compassion

In early January 1990, a few days before the great upheaval that transformed Romania, I went there with two of my brothers. We spoke with young people. At that dramatic time a young Romanian told us that, out of love of freedom for his people, he had gone to the point of risking his life. Speaking of the future, he added, 'Without forgiveness, without reconciliation, there will never be peace, never for Romania, never for Europe.'

That young man had realized something. Without forgiveness, is there a future for peoples that have been devastated? Without forgiveness, what future is there for each individual? Without peace, how can we build the human family across the earth?

In the fourth century, Saint Basil wrote, 'You come to resemble God by acquiring goodness. Fashion a merciful and kind heart in order to clothe yourself in Christ.'[28]

If we were to lose mercy, the inner fire of an inexhaustible kindness, what would be left?

Life is filled with serene beauty for whoever strives to love with kind-heartedness.

Only compassion allows us to see others as they are. When we look at them with love, we discern in each person the profound beauty of the human soul.

If compassionate hearts were at the beginning of everything ...

If the love that reconciles became a flame burning within us ...

... around us would shine, whether we knew it or not, a Gospel transparence ...

... and these words would be illuminated from within: 'Love, and say it with your life!'

Love and say it with your life

From the early years of our community it has seemed essential that some of our brothers go to share the life of the most destitute. For example, a few of our brothers have been living in Bangladesh for over thirty years.

They live in great simplicity, eating only rice and vegetables, with an egg or a piece of fish once a week. Often they invite the poorest to share a meal with them. They welcome and support the disabled, and make sure people who are ill get the necessary care. They help the young people of the country take responsibility for the very poor, among other things by helping run little schools for children. From the outset they have established a trusting relationship with Muslim believers.

Many years ago, one of my brothers and I went to visit that small group of brothers in Bangladesh. Arriving in front of their poor dwelling we came upon a one-year-old child, wearing some rags, clinging to his brother who was not much older. Those two children were waiting for us. Taking the younger one in my arms, I noticed that he was stiff with cold. First we entered the tiny chapel to pray. I kept the child in my arms during the meal. Gradually he warmed up and finally he was able to take some food. Children begin to live again when they sense that they are loved and taken care of.

My brothers and I talked together. Their presence there could seem insignificant. But, through it, we are not deserting some of the most misfortunate people of the earth. How would we keep going in Taizé if some of us did not live in the midst of the poorest in Asia, Africa and Latin America?

Why go to live in such conditions and remain for years and years, perhaps for an entire lifetime? Not to bring solutions, but above all to be a simple presence of love. Yes, to love and say it by the life we lead.

Peace begins within ourselves

'God is preparing for you a future of peace, not of misfortune; God wants to give you a future and a hope.'[29]

These words were written six hundred years before Christ.

Today, a great many people are longing for a future of peace, for humanity to be freed from threats of violence.

If some are gripped by worry about the future and find themselves at a standstill, there are also young people all over the world who are inventive and creative.

These young people do not let themselves be caught up in a spiral of gloom. They know that God did not create us to be passive. For them, life is not subject to a blind destiny. They are aware that scepticism and discouragement have the power to paralyze human beings.

And so they are searching, with all their soul, to prepare a future of peace and not of misfortune. More than they realize they are already making of their lives a light that shines around them.

A Glimmer of Happiness

It is not only the leaders of nations who build the world of tomorrow. The most obscure and humble people can play a part in bringing about a future of peace.

A Christian by the name of Ambrose, who lived in Milan a long time ago, wrote, 'Begin the work of peace within yourself so that, once you are at peace yourself, you can bring peace to others.'[30]

In human beings there can be impulses to violence. For trust to arise on earth we need to begin within ourselves, making our way forward with a reconciled heart, living in peace with those around us.

Peace on earth is prepared in so far as we dare to ask ourselves: am I ready to seek inner peace and to go forward in selflessness? Even if I am empty-handed, can I be a ferment of trust in my own situation, understanding others more and more?

There are those who are bearers of peace and trust in situations of crisis and conflict. They keep going even when trials or failures weigh heavily on their shoulders.

As I finish these pages a few weeks after the death of the beloved Pope John Paul II, I would like to say here that my heart remains full of gratefulness for the exceptional ministry of communion and peace that he exercised for more than twenty-six years. He awakened a hope in so many young people. Over a hundred journeys in most of the countries of the world were the clear expression of a soul attentive to prepare a future of peace.

Each person can begin to become, by his or her own life, a point from which peace radiates outward. When young people make an inner resolution for peace and trust, they sustain a hope that is communicated afar, always further afar.

On some summer evenings in Taizé, under a sky laden

with stars, we can hear the young people through our open windows. We are constantly astonished that there are so many of them. They search; they pray. And we say to ourselves: their aspirations to peace and trust are like these stars, points of light that shine in the night.

And so, for my part, I would go to the ends of the earth if I could, to express over and over again my confidence in the younger generations.

Praying in Silence of Heart

II

One hundred
prayers

Nothing is more responsible
than praying

Personal prayer is always going to remain simple. Do we believe that many words are needed in praying? No. There are times when just a few words, often awkward ones, are quite enough for us to be able to entrust everything to God, our fears and our hopes.

As we abandon ourselves to the Holy Spirit, we find a path leading from anxiety to trust.

In prayer, we are enabled to sense that we are never alone: the Holy Spirit sustains within us a communion with God, not for just one moment, but on into that life that has no end.

Yes, the Holy Spirit kindles within us a light. No matter how pale it seems, it awakens in our souls the desire for God. And that simple desire for God is already prayer.

Praying does not remove us from the world's preoccupations. On the contrary, nothing is more responsible than praying: the more we live a very simple, very humble prayer, the more we are brought to love and to express that by our lives.

A Path of Hope

Holy Spirit
enable us to bring peace
into places of opposition,
and to make visible
by our lives
a reflection of God's compassion.
Yes, enable us to love
and to express it by our lives.

Jesus our peace,
by your Gospel
you call us to be very simple,
very humble.
You give growth within us
to an infinite gratitude
for your constant presence
in our hearts.

Praying in Silence

God of consolation,
even when we feel nothing
of your presence,
still, you are there.
Your presence is invisible
but your Holy Spirit
is always within us.

Holy Spirit,
you fill the universe,
and you bring within the reach
of our fragile humanity
these Gospel values:
goodness of heart, forgiveness,
compassion.

A Path of Hope

God of every human being,
when we simply desire
to welcome your love,
a flame rises up little by little
deep in our souls.
Very fragile though it be,
it always keeps burning.

Jesus, our hope,
in you we find the consolation
with which God comes to flood our lives,
and we understand that,
in prayer,
we can bring everything to you,
entrust everything to you.

Praying in Silence

Holy Spirit,
you have a call for every one of us.
So come, prepare our hearts
to discover what it is
that you expect of each of us.

God of compassion,
disconcerted by the incomprehensible
suffering of the innocent,
we pray for those
who are experiencing times of trial.
Inspire the hearts of those
who seek the peace
that is so indispensable
for the whole human family.

A Path of Hope

Holy Spirit,
in you we are offered
a way of discovering this amazing reality:
God does not wish suffering
or distress for people,
he never creates fear or anguish in us,
God can only love us.

God of consolation,
you burden yourself with our burdens,
so that we can move forward
at every moment,
from anxiety toward trust,
from shadows toward light.

Praying in Silence

Jesus, peace of our hearts,
in our nights
as in our days,
in the hours of darkness
as in those of bright light,
you knock at our doors
and await our response.

Holy Spirit,
mystery of a presence,
you enfold us with your peace
that comes to touch
our inwardmost heart,
bringing us a breath of life.

A Path of Hope

God, you love us,
so no matter how poor our prayer,
we seek you with confidence.
Your love burrows a way
through our hesitations,
and even through our doubts.

Jesus our peace,
you call us to follow you
throughout our whole lives.
So, with humble trust,
we come to realize
that you are inviting us to welcome you
again and again, for ever.

Praying in Silence

Holy Spirit,
even when our words
hardly manage to express
our longing
for a communion with you,
your invisible presence
dwells within each one
and so a joy may be offered us.

God of merciful compassion,
enable us to find ways
of waiting for you in prayer
and of welcoming the loving gaze
with which you behold each one's life.

A Path of Hope

Jesus, our hearts' joy,
you pour out within us the Holy Spirit.
He comes to renew trust
deep inside us.
By him we understand
that the simple longing for God
restores our souls to life.

Holy Spirit, comforter,
come and breathe on the anxieties
that are capable of keeping us
far from you.
And so enable us to discover
the sources of trust
that are already there in our inmost hearts.

God of compassion,
by the Gospel
we can sense
that you love us
even in our most secret solitudes.
Happy those who abandon themselves to you
with trusting hearts.

Jesus, our trust,
within us you come
bearing a flame.
Feeble though it may be,
it is enough to sustain in our hearts
the desire for God.

Holy Spirit,
by your constant presence in us
you guide us
to give our lives in love.
And even if we sometimes forget you,
you bestow on us a joy.

Jesus of merciful compassion,
overwhelmed with trials,
you threatened no-one,
you forgave.
We too wish to know how to forgive
remaining
very simple of heart.

To whom else should we go, other than you?

For as long as we can go back in history, vast numbers of believers have known that, in prayer, God brings a light, a life within.

Long before Christ, one believer prayed: 'My soul longs for you by night, Lord; deep within me, my spirit seeks you.'

A desire for a communion with God has lain within the human heart from endless ages of time. The mystery of that communion touches the most inward, the very inmost depths of our being.

So we can say to Christ: 'To whom else should we go, other than you? You have the words that bring our souls to life.'

A Path of Hope

Christ of compassion,
you welcome us
with our gifts and our frailties.
And by the Holy Spirit
you liberate,
you forgive,
you guide us to the point where
we give our very lives in love.

God of all loving,
we long to be attentive
when deep within us
your call rings out:
'Onward, and may your soul live!'

Praying in Silence

Holy Spirit, consoling Spirit,
receive our very simple prayer
as we seek
to entrust everything to you
and to rejoice at what you accomplish
in our souls.

Christ Jesus,
give us resolute hearts,
hearts that, in simple prayer,
untiringly seek
to discover a communion
with God.

God of mercy,
the Gospel enables us to grasp
this good news:
no one,
yes, no one is excluded
from your love,
from your forgiveness.

Holy Spirit, inner light,
we would wish never to choose
darkness
but ever to welcome
a light coming from you.

Jesus, our joy,
you call us to follow you
and we realize that
your Gospel can transform
our hearts and our lives.

God of compassion,
we praise you for the multitudes
of women, men, young people,
who, all over the world,
seek to bear witness
to peace,
to reconciliation,
to communion.

A Path of Hope

Holy Spirit, consoling Spirit,
when we remain in your presence,
silent, at peace,
that is already prayer.
You understand everything about us,
and at times even a simple sigh
can be a prayer.

Jesus, Saviour of every life,
as the morning star rises in our hearts,
you shed light even on our doubts
and our hesitations.

Praying in Silence

God, you love
every human person,
and we yearn to live
a communion with you
day by day,
in silence and in love.

Holy Spirit,
filling the universe,
as a breath of silence
you tell each of us:
'Be afraid of nothing.
Deep within you
is the presence of God;
seek, and you will find.'

Jesus, peace for our hearts,
your Gospel comes to open our eyes
to the fullness of your love:
it is forgiveness,
inner light.

God of all loving,
as we seek you with confidence,
we wait
for even our inner contradictions
to open to the presence
of your Holy Spirit.

Holy Spirit,
you do not wish us
to be anxious,
you enfold us with your peace.
It prepares us
to live each day
as a day that belongs to God.

Christ Jesus,
you came into the world,
not to condemn the world
but so that, by the Holy Spirit,
we could live
a communion with God.

God of peace,
although we may be fragile
we are eager to follow you
along the way that leads us
to love
as you love us.

Holy Spirit,
mystery of a presence,
you say to each of us:
'Why be worried?
One thing alone is necessary:
a heart attentive
to understand
that God loves you
and always forgives you.'

Praying in Silence

Jesus our hope,
fragile and empty-handed we may be,
but we long to understand
that you always shed light
on the way that leads to God.

God of love,
by your Holy Spirit
you are always present.
Your presence is invisible
but you live in the midst of our souls,
even when we do not realize it.

Holy Spirit,
breath of God's loving,
our prayer may be very
humble,
yet by the Gospel
we understand that you are praying
even in the silence
of our hearts.

A contemplative way of looking

It is not too much, for the human beings that we are, to remain before God in contemplative waiting.

In such prayer, a veil is lifted from what in faith cannot be expressed, and the inexpressible leads to adoration.

God is also present when fervour evaporates, when feelings weaken. We are never deprived of God's compassion. It is not God who is remote from us, but we who are sometimes absent.

With eyes of contemplation, we perceive signs of the Gospel in the simplest events.

They discern Christ's presence in even the most forsaken human being.

They discover throughout the universe the radiant beauty of the creation.

A Path of Hope

Holy Spirit,
always you come to enfold us
in your peace.
and when within us dwells
a joy drawn from the Gospel,
it is capable of bringing us
a breath of life.

God, you love us,
and the contemplation of your forgiveness
becomes a ray of goodness
in the humble heart
that entrusts itself to you.

Praying in Silence

Jesus, peace of our hearts,
you call each of us
to follow you.
To whom should we go,
other than you?
You, Christ, have the words
that give life to our souls.

Praised be the Holy Spirit!
Present in the depths of our souls,
and consuming the hard things
in our lives
by the fire of that presence.

A Path of Hope

God of peace,
you strive to set within us
a Gospel joy.
It is there, very nearby,
ever renewed by the trusting way
you behold our lives.

Jesus, our hope,
your Gospel enables us
to sense that,
even in dark times,
God wants us to be happy.
And the peace in our hearts
can make life beautiful
for those around us.

Praying in Silence

Holy Spirit,
filling the universe,
you give growth within each one of us
to a life of communion with God.
And there, opening out, spring
goodness of heart
and a self-forgetting for the sake of others.

God of mercy,
you shed an unexpected light
within our souls.
By it we discover that,
while a portion of darkness
may remain in us,
there is above all in everyone
the mystery of your presence.

A Path of Hope

Jesus Christ,
we seek you as you behold us.
Your looking comes to banish
the pain from our hearts.
Then you say:
'Do not worry;
though I am invisible,
always I am with you.'

Holy Spirit,
you open us to a Gospel reality:
love that forgives,
so much so, that nothing is disastrous
except the loss
of the spirit of merciful love.

Praying in Silence

God of consolation,
by your Holy Spirit
you come to transfigure our hearts.
In the midst of our very trials
you give growth
to a communion with you.

Jesus, our hearts' joy,
you enable all
who live by your forgiveness
and compassion
to sense the greatest
of all certainties:
wherever there is mercy
God is there.

A Path of Hope

God, you love every human person.
When we realize
that your love
is forgiveness above all,
our hearts find peace,
and may even be changed.

Christ Jesus,
you have a call for each of us,
as you say:
Come, follow me,
and you will find a resting-place
for your heart.

Praying in Silence

Holy Spirit, consoling Spirit,
with you we discover
that we are never alone
and you sustain within us
a constant communion
with God.

God of all eternity,
we long to seek for you
amidst the silences of prayer
and live by the hope
discovered in the Gospel.

A Path of Hope

Christ Jesus,
by your Gospel we realize
that what counts above all
is compassion.
Grant us, then,
hearts full of goodness.

Holy Spirit,
when our hearts feel anxious,
you open a way ahead
for each of us:
it means entrusting our whole life
to God.

Praying in Silence

God of all tenderness,
in you we can discover
the meaning of our existence:
it is to give our lives
on account of Christ and the Gospel.

Jesus,
in the Gospel you tell us
not to linger
over things that have hurt us.
And your forgiveness becomes a miracle
in our lives.

God, as you love us
we long to go to your living springs,
in days of joy
and in days of pain.
There, by your Holy Spirit,
you speak to our hearts.

Holy Spirit,
you are in communion
with each of us,
not for just a moment
but for ever, on into the life
that knows no end.

Surrendering oneself to God

When our personal praying seems poor and our words awkward, we should not stop midway.

Isn't one of our soul's deepest desires to attain a communion with God?

Three centuries after Christ, an African Christian named Augustine wrote: 'A desire calling on God is already prayer. If you would pray without ceasing, never stop desiring ...'

A great simplicity of heart underlies and sustains a contemplative prayer. That allows us to surrender ourselves to God, letting ourselves be borne toward him.

This process of self-surrender may be sustained by simple songs, repeated over and over, such as: 'My soul finds rest in God alone.'

While we are working and while we are resting, such songs continue within our hearts.

In a life of communion of this kind, God, who remains invisible, will not necessarily address us in language that can be translated into human words. Above all, God speaks by silent intuitions.

In prayer, silence seems to be nothing special. Yet in that silence, the Holy Spirit may enable us to welcome God's joy as it comes to touch the depths of the soul.

A Path of Hope

Christ Jesus,
Saviour of every life,
you suffer with all
who experience hardships
and you always welcome
any who entrust to you
their own burdens.

Breath of the love of God,
Holy Spirit,
at times we are quite taken aback
to discover how close you are
to us.
To each one you say:
surrender yourself very simply
in God; your little faith is enough.

Praying in Silence

God of peace,
you love and you seek out
every one of us.
You consider each human being
with an infinite tenderness
and deep compassion.

Jesus, we long to live
by those words
you speak to us in the Gospel:
'My peace I leave you,
let not your heart
be troubled any more.'

A Path of Hope

Holy Spirit,
enable us to turn toward you
at every moment.
We so often forget
that you are dwelling in us,
that you are praying in us,
that you are loving in us.
Your presence in us
is trust and constant forgiveness.

Merciful God,
in the footsteps of the apostles
and of the Virgin Mary,
you are preparing us
to abandon ourselves in you,
in trust and in love.

Jesus, hope of our hearts, you dwell in us,
and by your Gospel
you tell each one of us:
'Fear not, I am with you.'

Holy Spirit,
mystery of a presence,
you always come to us.
You remain
in the very depths of our souls
and you awaken within us the expectation
of a communion with you.

A Path of Hope

God of all loving,
for each of us you wish
a Gospel joy.
And when we experience trials,
a way forward remains open,
that of abandoning ourselves in you.

Christ,
you penetrate into our inmost depths,
and there you perceive an expectation.
You know that, without having seen you
we love you,
and still without seeing you,
we give you our trust.

Praying in Silence

Holy Spirit, inner light,
you shine on the happy days
as on the troubled times
of our lives.
And when the light seems to grow dim,
your presence remains.

God of all eternity,
you love each one of us
without exception
and in your constant forgiveness
we discover peace of heart.

A Path of Hope

Jesus of compassionate mercy,
you enable us to transmit
to those around us
a flame of hope
by the trust of our hearts.

Holy Spirit, Comforter,
to us, the humble of the Gospel,
you have entrusted a mystery of hope.
Even when we are unaware of it,
it is there
sustaining our trust.

Praying in Silence

God of compassion,
as we hearken to your Holy Spirit,
we long to remain
trusting enough
to be able to abandon ourselves to you
in every situation.

Jesus our peace,
with our very little faith
we long to be attentive to you
as you tell us:
'Turn to God
and put your trust
in the Gospel.'

Holy Spirit,
breath of the love of Christ,
you are always present;
deep in our souls
you lay the trust of faith.

God of peace,
by your Holy Spirit
you enable us to cross
the deserts of the heart
and, by your forgiveness,
you scatter our faults
like the morning mist.

Praying in Silence

Jesus,
born poor among the poor,
you are God's humility
and you come, not to judge,
but to open a way
of communion with God.

God, you love every human person.
When we surrender ourselves to you,
we come to understand that
even what pains our heart
is made bright by the Holy Spirit.

Jesus, our trust,
we long to love you
wholeheartedly.
Grant us the daring we need
to keep renewing
over and over again
the gift of our lives.

Holy Spirit,
open us to trust
and to simplicity of heart,
so we can forget ourselves
and abandon ourselves in you.

He accompanies us

On the evening of Easter day, Jesus was accompanying two of his disciples on their way to the village of Emmaus. At that moment, they did not realize that he was walking beside them.

We too experience periods when we are unable to sense that Christ, by the Holy Spirit, is there close by us.

Tirelessly he accompanies us. He sheds unexpected light into our souls. Then we discover that, while a certain darkness may remain within us, there is above all else in each one the mystery of his presence.

Let us try to be certain of one thing! Of what? Christ tells each one: 'I love you with a love that will never end. I shall never leave you. By the Holy Spirit, I shall always be with you.'

A Path of Hope

For Christmas

God of peace,
at Christmas we discover,
following in the footsteps of the Virgin Mary,
that one of the Gospel's pure joys
is advancing toward a simplicity
of heart and of life.
With the little we have,
we long to welcome you
in silence and in love.

For the Epiphany

God of love,
in our darknesses
your presence comes to kindle
an inner flame.
On the day of the Epiphany,
we are able to realize that
it is not ourselves who create
that source of light,
but your Holy Spirit
who dwells deep within us.

For Palm Sunday

Christ Jesus,
like your disciples on Palm Sunday
we too need a joy
to help prepare us to bear,
with you, our own cross.
While you tell each of us:
do not be afraid,
take the risk of following me
again and again for ever.

For Holy Thursday

God of compassion,
our hearts and minds are like
dry ground thirsting for you.
Then you spread upon us your Spirit,
peace of the Eucharist
that brings us alive.

A Path of Hope

For Good Friday

Holy Spirit,
by your presence within us
today you prepare us
to perceive God's compassion
and to understand that God
can only give his love.

For Holy Saturday

God of all eternity,
even when all within us
is silence,
our hearts speak to you,
and pray,
and we abandon ourselves in you.

For Easter

Jesus,
like some of your disciples,
we sometimes find ourselves
struggling to understand
your risen presence.
But by your Holy Spirit
you live in us
and to each one you say:
'Come, follow me, I have opened for you
a way of life.'

For Pentecost

Christ Jesus,
in your Gospel
you assure us:
I will never leave you alone,
I will send you the Holy Spirit
to be support and comfort,
to enable you
to be in communion with God
day after day.

For the Transfiguration of Christ (August 6)

Holy Spirit,
you know our frailties,
but you come to transfigure our hearts,
so that our very darkness itself
can become
inner light.

For All Saints' Day (November 1)

God of loving mercy,
in the footsteps of the saints,
all the witnesses to Christ
since the apostles and the Virgin Mary
until today,
you are calling us
to be bearers of peace,
of trust and of joy
for those around us.

For the death of someone dear

Christ of compassion,
you enable us
to be in communion
with those who have gone before us,
who can remain so close to us.
They already behold the invisible.
In their footsteps,
you prepare us to welcome
a gleam of your brightness.

For the birth of a child

God of all tenderness,
you come and make of us
the humble of the Gospel.
We are so eager to understand
that the best within us
is built up by means of
a very simple trust,
that even a child can achieve.

For a baptism

God, you love us.
Baptized in the Holy Spirit,
we have for ever welcomed Christ.
And to each one of us you say:
'You are unique to me,
in you I find my joy.'

Unfinished Letter III

Note by Brother Alois, successor to Brother Roger as Prior of Taizé

The afternoon of the day he died, August 16, 2005, Brother Roger called one of the brothers and said to him, 'Note down these words carefully!' There was a long silence while he attempted to formulate his thinking. Then he began, 'To the extent that our community creates possibilities in the human family to broaden ...' And he stopped there, too exhausted to finish his phrase.

These words reflect the passion that inspired him, even in his old age. What did he mean by 'broaden'? He probably wanted to say: do everything possible to make more perceptible for everyone the love God has for every human being without exception, and for all peoples. He wanted our little community to bring this mystery to light, through its life, in a humble commitment with others. So we brothers wish to take up this challenge, together with all those who are searching for peace across the earth.

In the weeks before his death, he had begun to reflect on the letter that would be made public during the meeting to be held in Milan at the end of the year. He had noted some themes and some texts of his that he wished to take up again and work on. We have taken them just as they were in order to compile this 'Unfinished Letter', translated into 57 languages. It is a kind of final message from Brother Roger, which will help us to go forward along the road on which God 'broadens our steps' (Psalm 18:36).

Reflecting on this unfinished letter in the meetings held in 2006 both in Taizé, week by week, and elsewhere on different continents, each person can try to find ways of completing it by the life he or she lives.

Brother Alois

'I leave you peace; I give you my peace.'[31] What is this peace that God gives? It is first of all an inner peace, a peace of the heart. This peace enables us to look at the world with hope, even though it is often torn apart by violence and conflicts.

This peace from God also supports us so that we can contribute, quite humbly, to building peace in those places where it is jeopardized.

World peace is so urgent in order to alleviate suffering, and in particular so that the children of today and tomorrow do not live in distress and insecurity.

In his Gospel, in a dazzling intuition, St John expresses who God is in three words: 'God is love.'[32] If we can grasp only those three words, we shall go far, very far.

What captivates us in those words? The fact that they transmit this luminous conviction: God did not send Christ to earth to condemn anyone, but for every human being to know that he or she is loved and to be able to find a road to communion with God.

But why are some people gripped by the wonder of a love and know that they are loved, even to the point of fulfilment? Why do others have the impression that they are neglected?

If only everyone could realize that God remains

alongside us even in the fathomless depths of our loneliness. God says to each person, 'You are precious in my sight, I treasure you and I love you.'[33]

Yes, all God can do is give his love; that sums up the whole of the Gospel.

What God asks of us and offers us is simply to receive his infinite mercy.

That God loves us is a reality sometimes hard to comprehend. But when we discover that his love is forgiveness above all else, our hearts find peace and are even transformed.

And then, in God, we become able to forget what assails our hearts: this is a wellspring from which we can draw freshness and new vitality.

Are we sufficiently aware that God trusts us so much that he has a call for each one of us? What is that call? God invites us to love as he loves.
And there is no deeper love than to go to the point of giving oneself, for God and for others. Whoever lives a life rooted in God chooses to love. And a heart resolved to love can radiate goodness without limits.[34]

Life is filled with serene beauty for whoever strives to love with trust.

All who choose to love and to say it with their life are led to ask themselves one of the most compelling questions of all: how can we ease the pain and the torment of others, whether they are close at hand or far away?

But what does it mean to love? Could it be to share the suffering of the most ill-treated? Yes, that's it.

Could it mean having infinite kind-heartedness and forgetting oneself for others, selflessly? Yes, certainly.

And again: what does it mean to love? Loving means

forgiving, living as people who are reconciled. And reconciliation always brings a springtime to the soul.

In the small mountain village where I was born, near our home, a large poverty-stricken family lived. The mother had died. One of the children, slightly younger than I, often came to see us. He loved my mother as if she were his own. One day, he learned that they were going to leave the village and, for him, leaving was not easy at all. How can a child of five or six be consoled? It was as if he did not have the perspective needed in order to make sense of such a separation. Shortly before his death, Christ assured his friends that they would receive a consolation: he would send them the Holy Spirit who would be a support and a comfort for them, and who would always remain with them.[35]

In the heart of each person, Christ still whispers today, 'I will never leave you all alone; I will send you the Holy Spirit. Even if you are in the depths of despair, I remain alongside you.'

Welcoming the comfort that the Holy Spirit gives means seeking, in silence and peace, to surrender ourselves to him. Then, though at times serious difficulties may occur, it becomes possible to go beyond them.

Are we so easily upset that we need to be comforted? There are times when all of us are shaken by a personal trial or by the suffering of others. This can go so far as to undermine our faith and extinguish our hope. Rediscovering the trusting of faith and peace of heart sometimes involves being patient with ourselves.

One kind of suffering leaves a particularly deep impression: the death of someone we love, someone we may have needed in order to keep going forward here on earth. But such a trial can sometimes be transfigured, and then it opens us up to a communion.

A Gospel joy can be restored to someone in extreme distress. God comes to shed light on the mystery of human suffering, going so far as to welcome us into an intimacy with himself.

And then we find ourselves on a path of hope. God does not leave us all alone. He enables us to advance towards a communion, that communion of love which is the Church, at one and the same time so mysterious and so indispensable ...

The Christ of communion[36] offers us this enormous gift of consolation.

To the extent that the Church is able to bring healing to our hearts by communicating forgiveness and compassion, it makes a fullness of communion with Christ more accessible.

When the Church is intent on loving and under-standing the mystery of every human being, when tirelessly it listens, comforts and heals, it becomes what it is at its most luminous: the crystal-clear reflection of a communion.

Seeking reconciliation and peace involves a struggle within oneself. It does not mean taking the line of least resistance. Nothing lasting is created when things are too easy. The spirit of communion is not gullible. It causes the heart to become more encompassing; it is profound kindness; it does not listen to suspicions. To be bearers of communion, will each of us walk forward in our lives on the road of trust and of a constantly renewed kind-heartedness?

On this road there will be failures at times. Then we

need to remember that the source of peace and communion is in God. Instead of becoming discouraged, we shall call down his Holy Spirit upon our weaknesses.

And, our whole life long, the Holy Spirit will enable us to set out again and again, going from one beginning to another towards a future of peace.[37]

To the extent that our community creates possibilities in the human family to broaden ...

1. Luke 8:50.
2. Matthew 16:15.
3. 2 Timothy 1:7.
4. See Sirach 30:21–23.
5. Saint Augustine, *Confessions*, 12, 10.
6. Matthew 5:44.
7. See John 14:16–18.
8. *Taizé, A Meaning to Life*, Chicago: GIA Publications, 1997, p. 72.
9. See Luke 10:21.
10. See John 1:9.
11. See Matthew 5:3.
12. Luke 18:16.
13. Paul VI, Discourse at the closing session of the Second Vatican Council, December 7, 1965.
14. Matthew 25:40.
15. 1 John 4:8,16.
16. Isaiah 26:9.
17. Commentary on Psalm 37:14.
18. See John 6:68.
19. John 4:24.
20. Luke 23:46.
21. Commentary on Psalm 125:8.
22. Quoted in *Service Orthodoxe de Presse*, no. 282, November 2003.
23. Discourse of Pope John Paul II to the delegation of the Orthodox Church of Greece, March 11, 2002.

24. See Matthew 5:24.
25. During his visit to Taizé on October 5, 1986, Pope John Paul II proposed a road to communion by saying to our community, 'By desiring to be yourselves a "parable of community", you will help all whom you meet to be faithful to their church affiliation, the fruit of their education and their choice in conscience, but also to enter more and more deeply into the mystery of communion that the Church is in God's plan.'
26. Discourse to the parish priests of Rome, February, 1959.
27. Closing homily at the Second Vatican Council, December 8, 1965.
28. On the Origin of Humanity, I, 17 (Sources chrétiennes 160, p. 211).
29. See Jeremiah 29:11.
30. *Treatise on the Gospel of Luke*, V, 58.
31. John 14:27.
32. 1 John 4:8.
33. Isaiah 43:4.
34. At the opening of the Council of Youth in 1974, Brother Roger said 'Without love, what is the good of living? Why live any longer? For what purpose? That is the meaning of our life: to be loved for ever, loved into eternity, so that in our turn we go to the point of dying for love. Yes, happy those who die for love.' Dying for love meant for him loving to the very end.
35. John 14:18 and 16:7.
36. The 'Christ of communion.' Brother Roger already used this expression when he welcomed Pope John Paul II to Taizé on October 5, 1986: 'The constant longing of my brothers and myself is for every young person to discover Christ, not Christ taken in

isolation but the "Christ of communion" present in fullness in that mystery of communion which is his Body, the Church. There, many young people can find ways to commit their entire lives to the very end. There they have all they need to become creators of trust and reconciliation, not just among themselves but with all the generations, from the most elderly to little children. In our Taizé Community, following the "Christ of communion" is like a fire that burns us. We would go to the ends of the earth to look for ways, to ask, to appeal, to beg if need be, but never from without, always while remaining within that unique communion which is the Church.'

37. These last four paragraphs were spoken by Brother Roger in December 2004 at the end of the European meeting in Lisbon. They are the last words he said in public.